Turn the Page and Find Out

Becky Ances

BookLeaf Publishing

India | USA | UK

Presentation by *BookLeaf Publishing*

Web: www.bookleafpub.com

E-mail: info@bookleafpub.com

ISBN: 9789363307445

First edition 2024

To all the unwritten poems

Welcome

What makes a poem a poem?

What makes a poet a poet?

Is it the simple act of writing one and calling it such?

Does the will to make a poem make a poet?

Let's find out together.
Turn the page

Jet Lag

Awake.
3am
Might as well go to the beach
Watch a peaceful sunrise.

But as I enter the park I see…
Runners, slick with sweat
Girls with matching outfits and full makeup
taking photos
Children with giant sandcastle compounds
complete.

I realize I am late.
The day has started hours ago for most
Without me.

There is no peaceful sunrise here, just a chaotic
active morning.

But then the sun comes up.

Everyone is silent for a moment
Facing the same direction
Focusing on the same thing

And for a moment it is quiet. It is peaceful.
I'm not late at all. I'm just in time.

3

Midnight Fridge

I woke in the middle of the night.
Saw he left the kitchen light on.

Annoyed, I got up to turn it off.

But first, a quick peek in the fridge for a snack.
Feeling unwell I went to bed early, missing
dinner.
So I was peckish.

There, in the middle of the fridge was a plate
with dinner on it.
My dinner.
He even included a fork.

He didn't forget to turn off the light.
He kept it on.
To guide me.

Streets

5

Today a street cleaner stopped me to take a
picture of her while working.
I had seen this before
Cleaners taking pictures of each other.
Bragging right, I thought.
Or showing off to the boss.

But no.

Her phone had an app.
It showed
The time
Location
Her name
Assigned job.

It wasn't for fun, it was required.

As I took a photo of her slopping out a
port-o-potty I thought
No wonder this city is so clean.

Starbucks

The life of an American
Living in China
Seems exotic to others.

But as I sit here writing this
In Starbucks
Eating Dairy Queen

I don't agree

Poetry

It doesn't come naturally to me
Or easily

Is it just prose
Cut
Up
To look more

Profound?

Courage

For some it means climbing mountains
Running marathons
Jumping from planes

But for me it means
Going out in the heat
Making plans with friends
Agreeing a day early to play a sport

Because I never know if I'll have the energy to
see it through.

Being so sick
For so long
Changed everything.

Wander

I like to wander in my mind.
Sometimes it's like a forest, dense and thick,
which I need to bushwhack through,
Other times I find large empty rooms, and watch
the dust dance around the light shining through
the windows.
Then there are the libraries, with rows and rows
of books, all memories.
I pick them up and flip through them while
sitting in a plush leather chair
Some are written like illuminated manuscripts
with epic tales and gorgeous paintings
Others are thin, with barely legible writing and
half scrubbed thoughts.
I like to look through them all,
At random
Taking my time

I can wander in here forever
Finding new rooms
New places
Often explored or never explored
Never bumping up against any walls or exits

Graduation

I think inspirational speeches
Poems
Cards
Are wasted on graduates

Instead we should hold ceremonies for when you
turn 40
Remind people Who are stuck in patterns
Routines
Careers
That there is a big world out there
That what you carved out isn't permanent.

That when they are middle age they can still:
Reach for the moon and land amongst the stars
They need to be reminded of:
Oh the places they will go.

We should give 40-somethings ballots and
speeches to inspire them. Let then throw caps in
the air.

Graduates don't need speeches.
Adults do.

Because they also have their whole lives in front
of them.
But have seem to forgotten.

Why?

When I was a child I went through a phrase
Of asking Why

It drove my grandma nuts

"Put your shoes on, we have to go"
Why
"Come down, dinners ready"
Why
"Time to get ready for bed"
Why
It got to a point where she wouldn't even answer
me anymore.

Now as an adult I still continue to ask why
But silently.
In my head

Women are happy when they have children
"Why?"

You need a high paying career
"Why?"

Americans live in America

"Why?"

Just like one I was young I don't need anyone to answer for me. It's enough to ask the question.

Boxes

I reach back
To the truly dusty forgotten corner
Past the box labeled "lottery"
Under the box that says "artists in NYC"
And find the box I have pushed back here, trying
to lose it in the mess.

Even after all these years, the box is still
humming with energy.
I sit down and look at it, but don't dare to open
it.

I know what's inside:
A giant ball of yarn, tangled and tarnished.
I could open this box, start unraveling it, one
inch at a time. I could polish it until it gleams
once again.

Or I could burn it, unopened. I could burn all of
these boxes, down to ash.
To make way for something new.

Halfway

15

The journey is half over.
I hope you don't regret going on it with me.
The road, once dirt and winding, is getting more
solid, more straight,
Do you see it too?

But the road continues
So turn the page…

Jim

Are you disappointed when you find the truth of
your hero's?
When their magic and pureness crumbles under
the simple facts of their real lives?

Or doesn't it matter.

Can you just accept their gift of creativity and
creation without string attached?
Can the product be pure in the place of the
person?

This is a question I have to answer, sadly, often.
Yet I have no answer. Not yet.

Dragonflies

17

Today I saw a bunch of dragon flies swopping
about
And though
I could write a poem about that

But is that too cliche?
With their grace and beauty are they too
common a topic for poetry?
Along with butterflies, flowers and love?

What about flies? Mosquitoes? Does anyone
write poetically about them?

Mosquitoes

I see the grace of the butterfly
The beauty of a bird in flight
And I envy them
For having something I can never have

But I have something better. A secret, an ability.
I'm stealth
A ninja.
I can outwit and outfly them all.

I fly, I buzz, I get into tiny cracks and gaps
without my wings crumbling.
They can't.
I get right up to humans and let them try to swat
at me, disappearing right in front of their eyes,
perplexing them.
They can't.
I can live in the same dwellings as them my
entire life remaining completely undetected.
They can't.

My wings, teflon, thin but strong as steel.
My eyes, bulging, allowing me to see all
directions at all time.

Custom built not for beauty but for mastery, for
survival.

Wind speed or direction doesn't affect me. I go
where I want to
Called by no one other than my own will.

they all find me disgusting
Humans, insects, animals.
They look down on me.
But I eat what they expel

So who's the filthy one now?

Expressions

I love when humans put their expressions on
their faces.
So clear and obvious that even when you don't
know them, their personality, it's is like they are
saying words.

Is this the right direction?
I just wanna sleep
I'm so excited to see you.
This is awkward as hell.
I want to go home.

We have the ability to understand so much
Like watching a monkeys trying not to fall
asleep in while sitting in the hot springs
Looking identical to a student trying to not fall
asleep in class.

And you can't help but laugh when a child,
groggy from sleeps, wakes up in a Starbucks,
looking around confused.
"Where am I?"
Even if you hate kids.

As humans empathy is our gift.
And our curse.
And usually we try to turn away from it.

But when someone bends over, showing their
butt crack, and you catch a strangers eye and
smile knowing they have the same exact though
That's when it is fun.

Limerick Break

There once was a man from nantucket
And then what?

What the fuck is a limerick again?

Poetic Rain

Outside the rain falls
Drip
Drop
Plop

Inside I drink tea
Sip
Slurp
Slop

I guess I'm a real poet now.

Fitting it Together

Puzzles are made to be completed.
And yet when I slip that last piece in
I feel such a sense of accomplishment

Like I have achieved something no one else has
No one else is smart enough
Clever enough
Diligent enough

And yet if the puzzle company didn't sell
thousands of each puzzle they would go out of
business quickly.

So I know many people accomplish the same
feat as me
Possibly quicker
Possibly better

But I don't know them
So I'll continue on thinking it means something
important, profound, about me
Thankyouverymuch.

Identity

"Since teaching is your passion…" as student
began before I cut him off.
"It's not my passion." He looked at me
confused.
That's just one identity, A small part of me

Some people moo when they see me because I
am "the Moo-Cow Girl."
Others start talking badminton the second they
see me because I'm "Badminton Becky"
To others I am the "girl that lives in China" and
they ask me to explain things beyond my
knowledge
A precious few know me as a writer

At home, I am a child, where my mom cuts up
fruit to feed to me despite me being almost 50.
To my Chinese friends I am "Xiao Bing"
To my students I am "Teacher"
To English speakers I am "Becky"

YouTube fans assume I am playing a sport every
night
My Netflix account thinks I never leave home

I am all of these
It's true
But I'm also not.

We Did It

27

Finishing an goal feels good
Especially when it doesn't come naturally to me

But that's what you should do in life, right?
Try new things…
Be uncomfortable…
Be willing to suck…
And look foolish…

Mission accomplished